READING POWER

Famous American Trails

The Old Spanish Trail

From Santa Fe, New Mexico, to Los Angeles, California

Arlan Dean

The Rosen Publishing Group's
PowerKids Press™
New York

Published in 2003 by The Rosen Publishing Group, Inc.
29 East 21st Street, New York, NY 10010

First Edition

Book Design: Christopher Logan

Photo Credits: Cover, pp. 12, 13, 16 Denver Public Library, Western History Collection, images MCC-1809, X-31752, X-21765, X-32505; pp. 4–5 courtesy of the Bancroft Library, University of California, Berkeley; pp. 6–7 Joslyn Art Museum, Omaha, Nebraska; pp. 7 (top), 9, 17 (top), 20–21 © Jared Taylor Davies; p. 8 courtesy Kansas State Historical Society; pp. 10–11 © Corbis; p. 11 (top) Christopher Logan; pp. 14–15 © Ben Mangor/SuperStock Inc.; p. 15 (inset) © Hulton/Archive/Getty Images; p. 17 (bottom) Thomas Vennum Jr., American Folklife Center, Library of Congress; pp. 18–19 Library of Congress, Prints and Photographs Division; p. 19 (top) Nebraska State Historical Society; back cover © Eyewire

Library of Congress Cataloging-in-Publication Data

Dean, Arlan.
The Old Spanish Trail : from Santa Fe, New Mexico to Los Angeles, California / Arlan Dean.
    p. cm. — (Famous American trails)
Summary: Describes the Old Spanish Trail and the pioneers who settled in California.
Includes bibliographical references and index.
ISBN 0-8239-6480-9 (lib. bdg.)
1. Old Spanish Trail—History—Juvenile literature. 2. Pioneers—Southwest, New—History—Juvenile literature. 3. Southwest, New—Description and travel—Juvenile literature. 4. Southwest, New—History—To 1848—Juvenile literature. 5. Frontier and pioneer life—Southwest, New—Juvenile literature. [1. Old Spanish Trail. 2. Overland journeys to the Pacific. 3. Pioneers. 4. Southwest, New—History—To 1848. 5. Frontier and pioneer life—Southwest, New.]
I. Title.
F800 .D43 2003
979'.02—dc21

                                        2002000163

Contents

A New Trail West

In the first half of the 1800s, the land in what is now the southwestern part of the United States was first owned by Spain and then by Mexico.

Spain had many settlements in California.

There were settlements in California and New Mexico. A trail was needed to connect Santa Fe, New Mexico, with Los Angeles, California, so that goods could be traded.

Many fur trappers and traders tried to find a way through the deserts and mountains of the Southwest. Sometimes they followed small trails made by Native Americans. In the 1770s, Spanish explorers made several small trails west from New Mexico but never reached California. Others made trails east from California but never reached New Mexico.

Fur trapper at work

In 1776, Francisco Domínguez (fruhn-SIS-koh doh-MIHNG-gehz) and Francisco Escalante (ehs-kuh-LAHN-tay) set out to make a trail from New Mexico to California. They did not reach California, but many of the trails they used later became part of the Old Spanish Trail. This marker (above) honors their journey west.

Connecting the Paths

In 1826, Jedediah Smith was the first person to get from the Great Salt Lake to southern California by a land route. He used some of the paths made by the Spanish explorers.

Jedediah Smith was an American fur trapper and explorer.

In 1829, Mexican trader Antonio Armijo *(an-TOH-nee-oh ar-MEE-hoh)* was the first person to make a trip carrying goods from New Mexico to California and back. He led the first pack train along paths that would become the Old Spanish Trail.

Check It Out

American explorers named the trail the Old Spanish Trail because they thought Spanish people had made it. In fact, the trail was first opened for trade and used by Mexican people.

Great Salt Lake

Traveling the Trail

The Old Spanish Trail was about 1,100 miles long. It was a trail used mainly by traders. It was not a road for wagons. The trail passed through the present-day states of New Mexico, Colorado, Utah, Arizona, Nevada, and California.

Check It Out

Traders from New Mexico brought wool and cloth to California. There, they traded for horses and mules, which they took back to New Mexico.

THE OLD SPANISH TRAIL

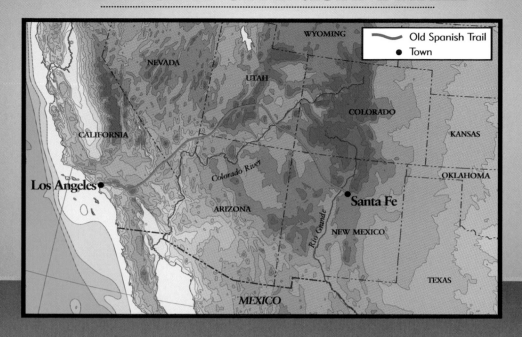

Old Spanish Trail
● Town

WYOMING

NEVADA

UTAH

CALIFORNIA

COLORADO

KANSAS

OKLAHOMA

Colorado River

Los Angeles ●

ARIZONA

● Santa Fe

Rio Grande

NEW MEXICO

TEXAS

MEXICO

Traders on the Old Spanish Trail had to cross the Colorado River in Utah.

Traders used horses and mules to carry goods along the trail. Traders often left New Mexico in the fall before the winter snows began. The trip back to New Mexico was made in the early spring before rains made rivers too deep to cross. It took traders over two months to make a one-way trip.

Traders got ready for their trip by tying supplies to a mule.

Check It Out

Pack mules, wearing iron shoes, often slipped as they made their way over rocks. Pieces of iron scraped from the shoes left marks on the rocks, which later rusted. The rust stains can still be seen today in rocky spots along the trail.

Parts of the Old Spanish Trail were very narrow. Mules, instead of wagons, were used to travel the trail. Pack trains, or mule trains, were sometimes as long as one mile.

13

The Old Spanish Trail twisted and turned. It crossed over land that made traveling hard. People had to either cross or get around plateaus, mountains, canyons, deserts, and rivers.

Near the end of the trail in California, people had to cross 50 miles of desert.

Parts of the Old Spanish Trail went through Mesa Verde (MAY-suh VUHR-dee), a large plateau in Colorado. An ancient city had been built into the sides of the plateau by early Native Americans. Mesa verde means "green table" in the Spanish language.

The Old Spanish Trail was used by traders between 1829 and 1848. Traders who used the trail would sometimes capture Paiute (PY-yoot) Indians who lived nearby. The traders sold the Paiute to other traders as slaves.

The Paiute lived in Utah, Arizona, and Nevada.

Some Native Americans, such as the Utes, cut pictures into the rocks along the Old Spanish Trail.

The Paiute used beads to make many different kinds of belts and necklaces.

The End of the Trail

In 1848, the United States won the Mexican-American War. The Mexican lands of California and New Mexico became part of the United States. Soon, the Old Spanish Trail was no longer used as the main way to get to California.

The U.S. Army fought many battles before winning the Mexican-American War.

After the Mexican-American War, people found easier trails for traveling from east to west.

Thousands of traders used the Old Spanish Trail to carry their goods. Many traders cut their names into rocks along the trail. These names can still be seen today. The names are reminders of the long journeys on the Old Spanish Trail.

Traders on the Old Spanish Trail traveled over 1,000 miles of wide open land.

The Old Spanish Trail Time Line

1770s	*Spanish explorers set out to find a path between Santa Fe and Los Angeles.*
1826	*Jedediah Smith reaches California by land.*
1829	*Antonio Armijo is the first trader to travel from New Mexico to California following the paths that become known as the Old Spanish Trail.*
1829–1848	*The Old Spanish Trail is used by traders to move goods between California and New Mexico.*
1848	*People stop using the trail after the United States wins the Mexican-American War.*

21

Glossary

canyons (kan-yuhnz) deep, narrow valleys with steep sides

explorer (ehk-splor-uhr) a person who searches for new places

goods (gudz) things, such as cloth, that are produced for sale

pack train (pak trayn) a line of mules carrying goods on their backs

plateau (pla-toh) a high, flat area of land that has steep sides

route (root) a way taken to get somewhere

settlements (seht-l-muhnts) places where people come to live

trader (tray-duhr) a person who buys and sells things

trapper (trap-uhr) a person who uses a trap to catch wild animals for their fur or meat

Resources

Books

Explorers, Trappers, and Guides
by Judith Bentley
Henry Holt & Company (1995)

The Royal Roads:
Spanish Trails in North America
by Kathy Pelta
Raintree Steck-Vaughn Publishers (1997)

Web Sites

Due to the changing nature of Internet links, PowerKids Press has developed an online list of Web sites related to the subjects of this book. This site is updated regularly. Please use this link to access the list:

http://www.powerkidslinks.com/fat/olst/

Index

Word Count: 525

Note to Librarians, Teachers, and Parents

If reading is a challenge, Reading Power is a solution! Reading Power is perfect for readers who want high-interest subject matter at an accessible reading level. These fact-filled, photo-illustrated books are designed for readers who want straightforward vocabulary, engaging topics, and a manageable reading experience. With clear picture/text correspondence, leveled Reading Power books put the reader in charge. Now readers have the power to get the information they want and the skills they need in a user-friendly format.